Monkey's Blood

Understanding Your Destiny

By

Larry A. Yff

CHAPTERS

1. The Evolution Theory   4

2. The Big Bang Theory   12

3. The Creation Story   18

4. Theory Face-Off   28

5. The Problem with God   32

6. Discover Your Destiny   44

7. Private Matters   48

ACKNOWLEDGEMENTS

I want to thank God for giving me another opportunity to use the skills He has given me to help people discover their destiny. To the world education system: thank you for trying to push the Evolution theory and the Big Bang theory on us, because it helped us open door #3 and the key to finding our destinies...the Creation story. To those who don't believe in God: you will appreciate this book even more because it's based on common sense...not religion. We are all humans and we all have value.

CHAPTER ONE

The Evolution Theory

It's important to look at the evolution theory for a number of reasons. One reason is to figure out why the world education system includes it as mandatory learning and the other reason is because if it's true, your destiny and mine will be revealed. Our purpose will come from understanding how humans came to be from animals and what our role is on this Earth.

The evolution theory tells us humans came from monkeys. The foundation of this theory has no foundation. Let's take a closer look. According to evolution theorists, in the beginning there was no life on Earth except for a one cell *being* that lived in water.

This theory starts with no suggestions as to how Earth became the way it was. It simply assumes...well, it doesn't actually assume anything because it doesn't address the actual origins of Earth OR life on Earth. But to continue our analysis of evolution, we will have to start where they start and that's with half the story. Eventually, this one cell being would split in half and continue to split and multiply. Some of these *water beings* would evolve into some type of land animal; while others were content with living in the water. This brings up another whole host of questions. Question One: do evolutionists want us to believe all sea creatures have the same genetic origin? And Question Two: do all land animals have the same genetic origin?

If that assumption is true, that would mean the simplest of sea animals and whales come from the same stock. This theory would have us believe the one cell *water being* evolved from being a shrimp to becoming 10-ton whales. I am not a water scientist (or whatever their technical name is), but if I were to ask one of them if shrimp and whales are related they would say no.

This also means we have to take a look at the beginnings of land animals according to this theory. This is where I will spend a little more time because evolutionists find it extremely rationale and natural that some frogs would eventually turn into humans while other frogs will turn into horses.

In the beginning there were frogs (or some other simple being fresh out the water with lungs). How many animals can you name that used to live in water but are now land animals? Evolutionists may point to the 1 out of 10,000 water species that has actually adapted gills and lungs and can function on both land and in water as their proof.

Those are not good numbers, my friends. That would kind of be like a person who decides to make playing the lottery their source of income for life. "Hey, you never know...remember that one guy who defied the odds and won the lottery? That could be me!"

If what they say is true, those of you who have fish as pets need to be careful because somewhere in your little goldfish's DNA is the genetic drive to evolve into a land animal. Do you get the picture? Let me go a little further with this example. You may come home one day and find your goldfish dead outside of its bowl because it felt the natural, genetic drive to live outside of its natural habitat. THAT is what evolutionists want us to believe.

In that same line of reasoning, beaches could eventually be littered with dead whales and dolphins who are literally dying to escape their natural habitat in an attempt to satisfy a drive to be a land animal. I think it's fair to say common knowledge is fish and water animals tend to want to stay in their natural habitat and not venture too long out of it if at all.

Land animals. Evolutionists want us to believe all land animals are related. They must not never have watched National Geographic. Predators are born with fangs and claws and love to kill grass-eating animals. They have all the necessary weaponry to carry out that task. Their stomachs are even made to digest meat in a timely manner.

That being said, I am having a hard time seeing how lions and deer evolved from the same being? Typically, the only answer to "how" and "when" is that evolution could possibly maybe have done this over one million or a gazillion years. Whatever the biggest, most speculative, mind-blowing number evolutionists can give us…they will. In their eyes, by telling the world it took a gazillion years for this evolutionary process to happen should satisfy further questioning; because they did in fact give us a pretty definite time frame: a gazillion years or so.

Once again, we have to slow down and dissect this theory and expose it for the nonsense it is. What evolutionists are clearly saying is that the original, one-cell *water being* had the makings of both a deer and a lion in its genetic DNA.

You know me: let's take this example a little further for more clarity. When two lions, for instance mate, according to evolutionist the possibility is there that a lion cub with a pre-disposition to being a grass-eating herbivore may pop out the lion mommy's womb. Nonsense.

Now let's get down to business and talk about monkeys. This is the evolutionists pride and joy of examples and proof that humans are no more than monkeys who flipped their genetic switches and decided to become human.

I will admit monkeys are the closest animal to a human I have ever seen. They have the five fingers with finger nails. They can take a banana and peel it like a human would and they can even walk upright. I have even seen humans participating in "monkey business" and other shenanigans. That's about as far as I can take it. How someone can make the jump that an animal that can eat fruit like a human must be a human is beyond me.

Here's where your understanding of evolution and your destiny meet: if you believe you are no more than a super monkey, then you have no destiny. You are an animal by nature. It's in your blood. You have monkey blood running through your body. Your destiny no longer is special, rendering you non-special. Your way of thinking, loving and all other actions are all primal and self-centered like your typical animal. Do you believe that?

I said this book is based on logic and I will try my hardest to not incorporate anything religious in here. I want to appeal to your sense of logic and reason. If you fall for the theory of evolution, you might as well be dead. Literally. Your purpose here on Earth as a human is not an awe-inspiring experience. You have no more responsibility to take care of this Earth or to love your fellow humans than a monkey does. You have nothing to live for other than to eat, sleep, shit, reproduce and die…just like your German Shepard (or labra-doodle). Let that be a wake-up call for anyone trying to find their purpose who believes in evolution.

CHAPTER TWO

The Big Bang Theory

This theory, unlike the evolutionary theory, provides an explanation for the beginning of the Earth...but leaves out the other half which is how life got here. These theorists believe it is normal for law and order to come from chaos. They must not have a yard. Anyone knows when you leave nature to itself, the grass will grow. Left to its own vices, your yard will naturally grow into an unruly mess of grass, weeds, small trees, moss, vines and anything else that feels like growing there.

In the beginning was a big ass explosion that resulted in Earth being formed. Just saying that doesn't make much sense; but in the true nature of democracy, I have committed to giving all the Earth-forming stories equal space.

Have you ever seen an explosion? If so, have you ever seen an explosion that resulted in a beautifully orchestrated thing of beauty? And I'm not talking about you weekend Destructicons who like to watch stuff get blown up. Everything that gets blown up is a thing of beauty to you.

Big Bang theorists would have us believe there was an explosion and the result was a thing of law and order. That the result of a violent bang created a planet with just the right amount of gravity and distance from the Sun that life as we know it could exist. Imagine that. Somehow, after the explosion, all the pieces had roundish shapes (planets) and different galaxies were naturally formed. This chaotic bang somehow defied every law of nature known to mankind and yet, these theorists want us to believe it.

The galaxy we live in is called the Milky Way. The common scientific evidence shows we have 9 planets in our galaxy. Some planets have multiple moons that orbit around it; while others like Earth have one moon. Are we so stupid to believe an explosion resulted in our galaxy having 9 planets, each in its own orbit around a central star called the Sun, each with its own moon(s) orbiting around it and they have never crashed into each other? Are we to believe these planets just happened to fall magically and perfectly in life to form our galaxy? Are we to believe the Earth just so happened to be the perfect distance from the Sun to prevent the world from freezing or burning up?

Hold on because I can do this all day long, so bring a lunch and sit tight (maybe even bring some dinner). These theorists want us to believe every galaxy out there just so happened to form around a central star like ours? Scientists have discovered thousands of galaxies, each with its own space boundary. So, are we to believe an explosion can result in all that law and order naturally?

When you blow something up, the resulting pieces reflect the object that was blown up. Let me put it to you a different way. If you blow up a potato in the microwave, you can expect to see pieces of the potato core and skin everywhere in no particular order.

Here's how that illustration relates to the Big Bang theory: an explosion sent planets to every corner of space and somehow only one planet ended up with water, trees, life and a protective ozone layer? There are millions of planets out there that are supposed to be the result of a massive explosion and only one somehow had life on it. There should've been fragments of life and ozone layer pieces evident throughout the Universe if a massive bang with one origin started life.

Since I am not a space scientist (or whatever they are called), my understanding of stars, black holes and planetary matters is pretty slim. That being said, I have a whole lot of common sense, and even that is said to be pretty slim...regardless, me and my low level of understanding of space matters knows the probability of life as we know it originating from a big bang has less chance than the theory that a one cell *water being* somehow evolved into every single animal and human life form on the planet.

I said this book is based on logic and I will try my hardest to not incorporate anything religious in here. I want to appeal to your sense of logic and reason. If you fall for the big bang theory, you might as well be dead. Literally. Your purpose here on Earth as a human is not an awe-inspiring experience.

You have no more responsibility to take care of this Earth or to love your fellow humans than a monkey does. You have nothing to live for other than to eat, sleep, shit, reproduce and die...just like your German Shepard (or labra-doodle). Let that be a wake-up call for anyone trying to find their purpose who believes in the big bang.

CHAPTER THREE

The Creation Story

This view of life on Earth is based on the belief that there is some other life form *out there* other than humans and they are responsible for creating the Universe. This view also has its fair share of skeptics because in order to believe in it we must have faith. In other words, believing that the Universe was made by some life form that we cannot see or comprehend, is the foundation of the Creation story.

There are a couple of things this view addresses that the other views have no logical answer for. These points are how the Earth was made AND how life began. The other views addressed either how Earth was made OR how life began.

How the Earth was made. When you look at nature, you can't deny the natural order of things. There are laws in nature that are unchangeable. There is also a sense of togetherness or planning when you step back and take a bird's eye view. Let's take that view for a second.

Ok, we are looking down at nature and observing. We notice there is water. Some water is more stationary than other, meaning some comes from the sky while other water is naturally contained in the forms of lakes, rivers and streams. Regardless of its classification, water was here from the beginning and without it, there would be no plant or human life.

Imagine no water here. Water provides nourishment for trees. Trees provide food such as oranges, apples, peaches and pears as well as performing an air-cleaning process called photosynthesis. What that is a process where trees "inhale" chemicals and toxins in the air and "exhale" air that humans and animals can breathe. Without trees and this process the air would be unbreathable and life would not exist on this planet.

Water also is necessary for all plant life to grow. Introduce a gazelle. A gazelle is a plant-eating animal that is also the main food source for meat-eating animals like lions. It's a natural process where grass grows, the gazelle eats it and grows then a lion eats the gazelle and it grows…in the end the all die and become plant and the process starts all over again. But remember, this does not take place if water was not here. Water therefore is an essential part of a plan for life on just this Earth.

I want to take a quick timeout to say water is not available on any other planet. Remember, there are millions of planets we have discovered and scientists are saying there are sectors of space that we haven't had access to that most likely hold millions more. Out of all these planets, only one, good ole Mother Earth, has water. Doesn't that stand out just a little bit? Doesn't it kind of seem like this planet called Earth is special? Doesn't it seem like there is some kind of plan for this Earth that separates it from the millions of other planets in our Universe?

Let's look at nature a little more before we dig into human life. There is a thing called a bee. Bees fly around and collect pollen from plants. If bees did not perform this process, we would not have fruit. It's as though there is a plan in place to design a specific insect to perform a specific duty to make sure food trees and all other pollenated plants exist. Without these plants humans would have no vegetation in their diets.

Taking vegetation a couple steps further...a diet without vegetation results in health deficiencies for humans. We HAVE to include vegetation in our diets. Carrots provide Vitamin A. Oranges provide Vitamin C. Bananas provide Vitamin K and the list goes on. The majority of illnesses, and subsequently natural cures, can be traced to the level of vegetation in one's diets. It's as though there is a plan for vegetation to exist so that human life can exist.

Now we get to introduce life into our bird's eye view. The human body consists of water in amounts as high as 70%. What does that mean for humans? It means water is imperative for life. It means humans cannot live on a planet without water. It means Earth is the ONLY planet humans can live on. I'm not sure what the water percentage is for plants and animals, but I can guarantee there is not one plant or animal that can live without water. Translated in another way: plant, human and animal life CANNOT live on any of the millions of planets in this Universe except for Earth.

The creation story provides us with an explanation for how the Earth was made. Based on all the logic and planet we see in nature, creation story believers believe in the presence of an unseen being...3 to be exact. They believe this being is God. They believe God has a son named Jesus and they believe there is another being who is identified as the Holy Spirit who rounds out what is known as the God-head or Trinity.

According to creationists, God Himself made the Universe. The logic behind this story is this: with all this planning in nature and life there HAS to be some type of logical being who has the ability to understand the future in the past, present and future sense. The planning of the Universe suggests there HAS to be some thinking being or beings behind it. This is the main point that separates the creation story from the two previously mentioned approaches: there is an acknowledgement of a more powerful, more intelligent being present throughout the Universe.

The story of creation has been passed down in a book called the Bible. This book gives us the headlines: God made the Earth and the Universe in 7 days. On days 1-5 He made the Earth, stars and all the other outer-space elements. On the 6th day, God, along with Jesus and/or the Holy Spirit, made man. The story also says man was created in God's images; which leads us to believe we somehow resemble our creators.

Let's switch gears from how the Earth was formed to how life began. On the 6th day, according to the creationists, God and/or Jesus and the Holy Spirit made humans. Here is where there is another huge difference between this view and the other two theories: an explanation of how life began on Earth.

The Bible says God made man from dirt. This makes sense actually. Think about this: when someone dies, the body is completely biodegradable. In other words, your body is composed of all natural components that eventually disintegrate back into dirt. In order for that process to be possible, humans would've had to have been made from dirt.

Remember we were talking about water? The human body was not designed to function without water. The human body was also not designed to function without vegetation. I covered that earlier, but I wanted to circle back around it because it ties in the creationist's story that human life was not just by chance: it was part of a plan.

After creating a man, God created a woman. This makes sense as well: there are two distinct species of humans designed for distinct purposes. When you look at a man, he has, well, I am going to be blunt: the man has a dick, balls and testosterone. *That* tri-fector is what makes a man a man. His brain is programmed to have a body with those parts. The testosterone gives him the aggression to thrust his body part into a female and release his seed from his balls. That process is called creating life. Creationists say that is one of the things God told man to do as part of a man's purpose.

On the other hand, the woman has titties, a va-jay-jay, flexible hips, estrogen and a uterus. Her brain is designed to function on a different level. When it comes to reproduction, her mentality is to entice. She's like a store that needs to advertise to attract the attention of shoppers to "enter".

Her hips are flexible and to accommodate the formation of a baby in her uterus. She has titties that naturally produce milk for nourishment for the baby. Her brain is naturally wired for the excitement of such actions. I don't know of any man whose brain is hardwired to want a baby coming out of his body parts or to have expanding hips.

Creationists believe God created human life in two species for specific purposes. These purposes are not limited to reproduction. There were other marching orders from God to have dominion and control over the Earth and all the animals. Have you ever seen a smart animal? I have.

I saw an experiment where a box with a latch-lock door was placed in the wild. Lions approached it and basically tried to eat it or throw it around. Curious elephants wanted to stomp on it…not the hyena. A couple of hyenas kept walking around the box and eventually figured out how to get it open and get the piece of meat out of it. My point is: I have NEVER seen an animal smart enough to control humans. Not a smart monkey. Not a smart rhino. Nothing. There is not an animal on the planet that has the ability to get together and make electricity, indoor plumbing or a housing development. There is no animal smart enough to control humans in any way, shape or form. WE do all the controlling around here...you better ask somebody.

CHAPTER FOUR

Theory Face-Off

Here's where we do a side by-side comparison of the different views on creation. We will not be able to look at every single point, but we will take a look at the headlines. They are as follows: the common-sense test and the reality test.

First up is the Evolution theory and common sense. How much sense does it make that a frog and a whale have the same genetic make-up somehow in their DNA's? Does it make sense that some monkeys evolved into humans while other monkeys preferred to stay a monkey? With those two examples, I would say the evolution theory flunks the test of common sense.

Let's look at the reality test for evolution. Based on the two examples I just gave, how realistic is it that a dog can trace its origins back to a frog or some other one cell being? I would say not very realistic at all, and that means evolution also flunked the reality test.

Next up is the Big Bang theory and common sense. Does it make sense that you can have an explosion and somehow wind up with hundreds of distinct galaxies that just so happen to have a sun in the middle that just so happens to be the right size with planet Earth just so happened to be the perfect distance from it for life to live on?

I would say the Big Bang theory flunks the common-sense test; unless you have seen an explosion where everything somehow fell neatly in order.

Let's look at the reality test for Big Bang theorists. How realistic is it that there was a huge explosion, sending millions of huge, planet-sized chunks of mass called planets across the Universe and somehow, Earth is the only one that had an ozone layer around it. How did that ozone layer even get there?

Because there are too many unanswered and impractical conclusions for the Big Bang theory, I would say it also flunks the reality test.

Last but not least is the Creation Story. How does the Creation Story perform on our common-sense test? Common sense says the Earth and the entire Universe has some type of planning. You may not agree that it was God like the Bible says; but at the LEAST, you have to agree nature cannot possibly have that many coincidences. That being said, the Creation Story shows at least beyond a reasonable doubt, there is proof of logic, law and planning in nature that is above the paygrade of any human or animal.

That proof shows beyond a reasonable doubt that something or someone had to have done that planning. The Creation Story presents God as that Designer. This basic acknowledgement of Creation's design, and therefore a need for a designer, says Creation Story passes the common-sense test.

Let's look at the reality test for creationists. The reality is, life was planned. The reality is, this planet was designed and set apart from millions of planets specifically for life. The reality is, humans are the dominate species on this planet. The reality is, humans are hard-wired and built to have dominion over everything and every other life form on this planet and that coincides with the Creation story.

Based on those facts, the Creation Story shows at least beyond a reasonable doubt, that the reality is humans, not animals, have complete control over this planet (with the exception being natural events such as rain, snow, etc.). The Creation Story passes the reality test.

CHAPTER FIVE

The Problem with God

As you know by now, I believe in God, Jesus, the Holy Spirit, the Bible and yes, the Creation Story. For me to write a book with comparisons on the three main creation theories and make the Creation Story come out on top smelling like roses would at first glance appear to biased. I can say that and I can see how some people could say that.

With that author-biased view lingering in the air, allow me to make some confessions: there is a lot I don't know about Creation and God. I don't have all the answers as to how God created the Earth as well as how the other two theories are absolutely not true.

What I have been able to show is the many, in-your-face, obvious flaws Evolution and the Big Bang theory have. What I didn't go into much detail about is the areas where flaws can be perceived in the Creation Story.

Since the Creation Story is based on God, who God is needs to be examined. To tell you the truth, it was difficult at first to put all my eggs in my destiny-basket based on the theory that some unseen being named God created the Earth.

That was until I studied the books in the Bible and the books that didn't make the cut for the Bible. In all of the books we have eyewitness accounts from people who are all unrelated and are from different time periods all saying they had some type of contact and communication with God.

None of them ever claimed to have seen God except for one. His name was Moses and his reputation is stellar and there is historical proof of his existence on Earth from the Bible as well as sources outside of the Bible.

You may think that is more proof that believing in God, a being who is documented and recorded all throughout history but never seen, is an impractical option. Nothing could be further from the truth. All of the recorded documents offer solid evidence of God's existence and that is all that is needed to be made known.

The various authors of the Bible had different careers and different walks of life that they claim were affected by God. When you have these authors, along with thousands of others who were witnesses to the acts of God but didn't write them down in books, you have a pretty strong case that God exists.

You don't need to have proof that you've seen something or somebody in order for that person or thing to be real. Have any of us seen the wind? No, we haven't, but we have felt it and seen how it affects things in our physical world.

That is similar to the proof I needed to see about God: if I apply the laws that have been passed down for thousands of years as being from God, will my life be affected by this unseen being just like unseen wind affects physical things?

Yes. I have personally applied the teachings and laws from the Bible that the authors have claimed come from God and my life has been affected exactly how they said it would. Have I ever seen God? No, *however*, my experience with Him has been exactly how they described their experience with Him.

Once I was able to see the practical implications from an unseen force or being, it was an organic and natural move to go from unbelief in the unseen to a position of belief that there are things we humans don't see that are somehow able to communicate with humans on both a spiritual and physical level.

Just because I was able to relate to this unseen being on a level similar to thousands of others who have claimed the same thing does NOT mean this being created the Earth and every other seen and unseen *things* out here…but it does act as more supporting evidence that 1) God exists and 2) since He exists and is able to design a plan for our lives in both the natural and unnatural, He is an excellent candidate for being the Designer behind creation.

I really was hard on the Evolution and Big Bang theories. I shot them the fuck up! Since I was hard on them, I will dig a little deeper into the being I say is responsible for creation and put Him under the microscope.

Once you say you believe God created everything, people tend to want to go on the offensive and attack His ability. They don't want to attack His existence, because there is a thing called faith that nobody can deny as well as the tons of evidence that 1) there is a spiritual realm that we cannot see and 2) beings that operate in this realm can operate in the physical realm as well. To try and start a debate as to God's existence would be an uphill battle.

The "better" option of non-believers has been to accept, or at least acknowledge, the existence of God and then begin to point out holes in how he has been known to operate. By pointing out supposed discrepancies in the Bible, they believe they are able to say, "Yes, God exists and yes, it's possible that He did make the Earth BUT He is not one to be followed because of all His back-pedaling." Non-believers also feel like this approach attacks His deity-status and therefore, He is not someone to be followed, respected, revered or worshipped and life is better left to the guidance and governance of human institutions.

In all fairness to non-believers, I have to say I have come across some things in the Bible about God that have made me scratch my head.

One of these things is the fact that God gets mad. The church and the Bible teach us that God knows everything before it happens and, like the Creation Story says, God designed everything from the start to the finish. If that's true, why would God get mad? Why would He have any type of emotions? When you already know what's going to happen there is no need to be surprised or get angry.

If I knew who would win the Superbowl before it started, I wouldn't be mad if my team lost. Actually, if I knew how everything was going to play out, I would have no interest in the game. That also brings up another area of possible pause for thought because people throughout history that have written and testified about God all claim that God loves each and every one of us and is excited when we choose to follow Him. Why would that excite God if He already knew certain ones of us would choose to follow Him?

In order to address those questions, I have to refer to a story in the Bible. There was a man named Job. His story includes Satan asking God directly to be allowed to do whatever he could to Job and his possessions just to get Job to stop giving God glory and respect. God agrees and sets the boundaries for Satan's actions: do whatever you want to his possessions and health, but you cannot kill him.

As the story goes, Satan wipes out all of Job's wealth and kills Job's children. During this crisis, Job has some friends, as well as his wife, who offer him advice. They throw their two-cents in and get him to eventually question whether or not God really cares.

He never said He didn't love God. He never said he didn't want to give God worship. The farthest he did was to wish that he were dead and he also began to talk with God.

As he talked to God, he began to ask God why was this happening to him? He began to question a lot of things and was asking God for answers as though God was doing something He shouldn't be doing to Job.

God answers Job and tells him, "Who are you? I am the one who designed all of this and I can change my mind at will. If I do change my mind, once again, who are you? Do you know how the Earth began? Do you know how the stars stay in the sky? Do you know how everything in creation and the spiritual realm work? Have you ever commanded or seen angels?"

Basically, God lets Job know that there are things He has planned for Job's life and that He does not need to explain Himself or justify His actions to a human. A being who is known to not being able to live forever. A being who has no historically documented proof of somehow existing for thousands of years and operating outside of time.

Job winds up passing the test presented to him and God restored Job's wealth. Actually, Job's wealth was documented prior to the test as being massive BUT it was stated and documented that his reward for passing the test was that God somehow doubled the amount of wealth he had before the test as well as blessing Job with more kids.

And that story shows the extent of my questioning of God and who He is. There is enough proof of His existence and there is also enough physical evidence of Him somehow doing things in our physical realm that defy science, logic and natural reasoning.

With all that proof and evidence, who am I to question what God does, how God does it and why He does it? And that brings up another whole set of questions such as: Do I need to know exactly how God operates? Do I need to know exactly how He does it? Do I need to know why He does what He does? And lastly, do I want to spend my limited time here on Earth questioning and doubting God?

There are exceptions to this rule that have been documented and verified all throughout history. There are people who have said they wanted to live life one way and they were able to honestly credit God as the "thing" that changed their lives.

I won't go into a lot of detail in this book because I go through it more in "White, Confused, Black and Christian – the Autobiography of Larry A. Yff". I will say that my story is similar to a lot of those exceptions I just mentioned.

I was addicted to cocaine and porn. At one point I asked God to just take it away from me. He replied, "If I take it away and don't allow you to publicly and privately experience all of the pain and emotions related to addiction, I won't be able to use you to show people how they can make dumb ass decisions in life and still turn to me for the solution no matter how deep in shit they got."

I never planned on 1) growing up and being addicted to drugs and porn and 2) being the crash-test-dummy for addiction. I told God I accepted, as though I really was in the position to doubt the Creator's plan for my life, and from that day on, I never questioned any of the pain, depression and rejection I felt from addiction.

I began to view it the way God was viewing it and began to share my story through my books to help people be honest with themselves no matter what. Most people haven't gone through all the extremes and poor decision-making I have gone through hopefully; but if there are similarities, my openness and honestness have become part of my testimony and hopefully will be a part of your healing.

In the end it is up to you as an individual to decide how much proof do you need for the existence of God and once you find proof, how will this knowledge change your life? That's the beauty of life. We all have the freedom to choose our path.

CHAPTER SIX

Discover Your Destiny

Your understanding of your purpose, place and position on this planet is directly related to your view on the origins of life. If you think you were not planned or designed, you will believe life just happens and it is what it is.

Evolutionists want the world to believe that humans are animals. If we are animals, what kind of destiny can you expect to reach? Your answer lies in nature. You will have to find the highest form of intelligence in nature and make that your goal. I watch a lot of nature documentaries and have seen some pretty smart animals. I gave you the example of the hyena earlier. Do you want to achieve the goal of the hyena? Is your destiny simply to be able to think outside the box?

Some animals create families. Is that your destiny to be able to create a family? For some people that's all there is and when family is gone, they feel like they have nothing left to live for. Their reason for living is gone.

Some animals dominate the space humans let them live in. Is that what you want your destiny to be? Do you want to be the dominant being in your country or career? How many times have you seen someone trying so hard to get more and more and more money...only to die and leave everything they worked for behind on Earth anyways.

Most times these career-driven people are egotistical and to put it bluntly, they are pricks. Their family life tends to suffer and most times their sense of spirituality is so tainted it might as well be non-existent. If you were to take away their one claim to fame, whether it be money or fame, they would fall apart with a high probability of committing suicide.

The Big Bang and Evolution views on creation and life are either built from chaos, has no rules or views humans as being nothing. The lifestyle of those believers shows it. If you believe we came from chaos, you probably tend to believe the world is a chaotic place and can't be controlled. If you believe there are no rules or beings to be accountable, you will tend to live lifestyles that are full of confusion such as addiction-filled or self-centered.

The Creation Story is the one story that places humans above animals and below some other life form.

It is the only view that says we as humans were specifically designed to enjoy and dominate this place.

It is the only story that shows us everywhere we look that this world was designed for us.

It is the only view that at least offers a system of purpose and accountability.

It is the only system that passes the common sense and reality tests and it should be the only view for any rationale human being with common sense.

PRIVATE MATTERS

At the end of each individual book in the "Your View Matters" series is a section called Private Matters. It is a collection of short essays from my thoughts on things talked about in private that should be talked about openly. There are approximately 15 of these essays. Each book will typically have only the essays that relate to the subject matter of that particular book. What follows is that list for this book:

1. JESUS FREAK   49
2. A WOMAN'S WORTH   56
3. SPERM: THE ULTIMATE SEED   59
4. ONE NATION UNDER GOD??   62
5. A TALE OF THREE MEN   66

JESUS FREAK

There is a term thrown around called "Jesus Freak". It was designed to be a put-down on anybody who was seriously into Jesus. It worked. Well, it worked for a little while. I have to admit, it even worked on me...at first.

Following the Bible and being a Christian has always been a social and religious target for people who want to live life on their own terms. Nobody ever attacks Islam, Buddhism, Darwinism but if you mention you are a Christian or if you mention the name "Jesus", here come the sighs and the "why do you always have to talk about Jesus?" reactions.

Here's why. You know what? I was going to do it in paragraph form, but I just changed my mind. I like list's so I'm going to number some of the reasons why:

1. Jesus is the only human who ever claimed to know God directly and He had plenty of supporting evidence with His actions.
2. Jesus is the only human ever whose death was documented and witnessed by many people…and His resurrection was also witnessed and documented by many people.
3. Jesus is the only human that had documented records where He was able to tell storms to die down and to control nature.
4. Jesus is the only human who delivered a message that talked about getting personal with the creator of the Universe. All other religious and spiritual paths talk about some "thing" that is not designed for humans to get personal with (Islam being an exception…kind of).
5. Jesus is the only human who is recorded as performing actual miracles. Miracles that included raising people from the dead.

6. Jesus is the only human who gave us a clear explanation for human's purpose on Earth AND tied it into our spiritual origins. All other spiritual walks just tell us to do what we think is right and love everybody and we're gonna be A-ok.
7. Jesus is the only human who has recorded and documented manuscripts written thousands of years before His birth that predicted His coming.

I could go on forever with this list, but I won't. I think you get the point that Jesus was and is an extraordinary individual. He spent His adult life here on Earth looking out for us. His laser-focus was to let us know that God is real, Satan and sin are real and that since He is the only one who actually witnessed Earth's beginnings and the rise and fall of Satan and sin, His goal was to teach us how to duplicate the Kingdom of Heaven here on Earth.

He also had a ton of lessons about life that, if followed properly, will make any individual find peace, happiness and success in every situation in life. He tied right, wrong, good, bad,

God, Heaven, financial and spiritual wealth together in a way that no one before Him or since Him has been able to do.

If somebody wants to label me as a "Jesus Freak", I gladly accept that title. Actually, you can call me whatever the fuck you want to and I won't be offended or mad. In the case of the "Jesus Freak" label, I will actually shake your hand and thank you. That's a label I will gladly wear.

I have to say something about the "Jesus Freak" thing. A lot of people are finding it fashionable to wear bracelets that say "what would Jesus do" and people like to make social media posts that say "I love Jesus and He is My Lord and Savior. If you agree, please share." And now you got 3,000 mutha fuckas agreeing…but are they actually living like Jesus wants them to?

Do you remember the Lord's prayer? A lot of Believers say that prayer daily or at least a lot. How many of them understand that our purpose on Earth is to create Heaven on Earth? In that prayer, Jesus taught us to ask for "…may your Kingdom come…" That means we are asking for the Kingdom of Heaven to be established on Earth.

How does God work on Earth? Since He gave humans dominion, He rarely just comes in and does whatever He wants to do. He respects His own laws. What God looks for is for humans that He can work through.

The entire Bible if full of recorded events where God has Moses free the slaves, Joshua leading battles and prophets to give messages to world leaders and specific groups of people.

Jesus constantly told people who were interested in His lessons that they had to take action. Believers are supposed to suit up for spiritual warfare. Believers are supposed to stand up against laws that go directly against God's laws such as the legalization of homosexual marriage, corrupt and prejudicial drug sentencing laws and a host of other activity that certain members of society try and legalize so they can try and operate above God's laws.

A real "Jesus Freak" is ready to stand up when the rest of society is bowing down to social pressure. A "Jesus Freak" is an individual who doesn't just wear a *Jesus t-shirt* while he or she is actively involved in activities that destroy our temple such as drinking, vaping and letting their bodies get completely out of shape.

I will close with this: "Jesus Freaks" are the true leaders of society. Don't try and wear this badge without putting in the time. Being a "Jesus Freak" is not designed to be a fad. It involves daily prayer, meditation and conversations with our Heavenly Father, with Jesus and with the Holy Spirit. The key word is "daily". A true "Jesus Freak" does not go to church one hour a week and think that their "God time" quota for the week is satisfied. You don't get to wear the "Jesus Freak" label if that's the only time you tryin' to put in.

"Jesus Freaks", it's time to run shit!!! It's time to stop being scared to stand up for shit!!! It's time to stop letting human governments that contradict Heaven's government to continue to fuck shit up!!! It's time to re-claim your lost shit!!! It's time to start a local Bible Fight Club!!! It's time to do whatever your "Jesus shirts" are telling the world that you do!!!

LET'S DO THIS SHIT FOR REAL, JESUS FREAKS!!!

I'll see the rest of you freaks at the finish line!!!

A WOMAN'S WORTH

The Bible has several examples of how a woman can use her natural power and the results she can command:

Intentional use of Power: Jacob's mother used her female power of persuasion to help him deceive his father; Esther used her beauty and charm to become a queen and save her Jewish culture from genocide; the daughter of Herodias performed a sexual dance for the King who was so aroused by it that he told her she could have up to half of his kingdom; King David was about to kill a man and all the man's sons for disrespecting him but the man's wife stepped in and appeased David and saved her husband's life; God was going to kill Moses until his wife stepped in and did what God had wanted and that act saved Moses' life; and then there was King Solomon who asked God for wisdom over everything and in the end he allowed his wives to lead him astray to the point where he built temples for them to worship foreign gods and idols.

Unintentional use of Power: King David *looked* at a woman and wanted her so bad that he had her husband murdered; Jacob saw a beautiful female and told her dad that he would work for him for free for 7 years if he could marry her...he was tricked and forced to marry her older sister, but he went and told the dad he would *still* work for 7 more years if he could marry the younger sister who he wanted in the beginning; in Genesis it was told that the angels in Heaven *looked* down at the women on Earth and wanted them so badly that they would rather live on Earth and have them than live in Heaven; and finally, David had a son who lusted after his own step-sister so badly that he became physically sick and eventually raped her.

Understanding the worth of a woman and her role in a man's life is crucial, both from the man's point of view and the woman's. On several occasions God warned different men about their selection of a wife because if a wife doesn't love God, she has the power to lead her husband away from God. The first example of this was in the Garden of Eden. The apostle Paul says that sometimes it's best if a man stays single because a married man has a hard time pleasing God because of his strong, natural desire to please his wife. And at the same time, there

At the same time, the Bible mentions how a man should find a good wife because she will complement him and they will both be happy and powerful. In the Garden of Eden, Eve was created because God determined that Adam needed a female companion to complete him.

Here are some Bible verses that talk some more about a woman's worth:

1. Proverbs 11:16 – a kindhearted woman gains honor
2. Genesis 2:24 – a man will leave his parents to be with a woman
3. Proverbs 31:10-31 – a wife of noble character is: worth more than rubies, she has strength and dignity, gives good advice, helps the poor and deserves honor for everything that she does…
4. Proverbs 18:22 - Whoever finds a wife finds something that is good and receives favor from God.
5. Psalm 68:5 – God is a protector of widows

6. Exodus 22:22 – God says He will kill anyone who takes advantage of widows
7. Proverbs 12:24 – a disgraceful wife is like decay in her husband's bones
8. Proverbs 19:13 – a quarrelsome wife is like a constant drip from a leaky roof
9. Proverbs 29:3 – whoever messes with prostitutes will be poor
10. Proverbs 6:26 – an adulterous wife will cost you your life
11. Ecclesiastes 7:26 – thoughts of getting trapped by a woman are worse than contemplating death

In the end, a woman has the support life or death. She needs no weapons of war. Her mind, beauty and natural feminine qualities are her weapons of choice. How a woman follows instructions and where she gets her instructions from determines her worth and value.

The Bible: Basis Instructions Before Leaving Earth

SPERM: The Ultimate Seed

Sperm is the ultimate seed because of its power and ability to create humans.

1. Everything on this planet and in this universe was made for humans.
    - The ground and water provide natural nutrition for plants.
    - Through the process of photosynthesis, plants make the air breathable for humans and through consumption provide the human body with every necessary nutrient it needs.
    - Every human cell in our body needs water and without it, a human would typically die within 3-4 days. The chemical make-up of water, H20, makes water the only natural liquid that the human body needs to replenish itself and survive.
    - If the Earth was closer or farther away from the Sun...we would all die and if the Earth was to move faster or slower...we would all die.
2. Humans are the most powerful life force on this planet.
    - No other life form can control its environment like humans.
    - Nothing that is unnatural would have existed without humans: cars, boats, bridges, computers, etc.

- No other life form has the ability to manipulate every element on this planet to its will
3. On the spiritual side of things:
    - No other life form has a spiritual level comparable to humans
    - No other life form has the ability to control its spiritual destiny
    - Humans are the image of God

A man's body is the only life-form that produces semen, the seed of humanity. The following are some of the activities that are designed to weaken a man by stripping him of the proper use of his seed:

1. Lust
    - Masturbating/jacking is a waste of seed/power
2. Contraceptives/Safe sex
    - They are counterproductive to married couples because responsible, natural fatherhood truest form of natural power for a man
    - They kill the potential of the seed/life
3. Abortion
    - Destroys the females body
    - Kills the most powerful life form that exists

Seeds are important. Jesus said "If you have faith the size of a mustard seed you can move mountains." When God created the Earth, He told man "I give you every seed-

bearing fruit for you and the animals to eat." Every natural, living thing comes from a seed.

<u>For men</u>: You have power. Learn the correct way to plant your seed.

<u>For women</u>: You have power. Learn the correct way to select your seed.

<u>For parents</u>: You have power. Learn the correct way to nourish your seed.

The BIBLE: Basic Instructions Before Leaving Earth

ONE NATION UNDER GOD

The United States government is designed to distribute justice in its purest form at home and abroad. Our government has established itself as a military and financial powerhouse; but our political process is so full of corruption that it renders any thoughts of effectiveness null and void.

Our Constitution and legal tender both state that we are a God-fearing nation. In light of the fact that we define the protecting of our individual freedoms and rights as the enforcement of a separation between Church and State, can we truly be a God-fearing nation? The resulting, disturbingly high, level of inefficiency and corruption is the natural order of things. A government that claims to be fundamentally based on God-fearing principles and ethics while its hands are tied in regards to incorporating Biblical principles in its rulings is in essence a non-government.

The introduction of the "separation of Church and State" in our Constitution has become a declaration of this country's pious attitude towards God and religion. As noble as it appears to be, that one clause has proven to be the "writing on the wall" for America and has become the gateway clause to legally act and allow immoral actions by our governing bodies.

I do believe that this country's founding fathers had the right idea by creating a Constitution that by that time period's standards appeared to be morally correct. Including the reference to God gave it supernatural power, making it an instant gold-standard document. The Constitution now became a document that could be looked at as "being inspired by God." That reference was intended to be the undefined, moral DNA for all following pieces of legislation.

If America is to be truly great, it must shed its cloak of perceived morality. All evidence of it must be removed from our legislation with the same vigor we pursue terrorists, or civil rights violators or those who interfere with the economic interests of lobbyists.

One option is to just call it what it is and ban any reference to God on anything or any process that is government related; at least that way we as citizens know exactly what to expect and we can act accordingly. There are currently segments of society who are acting accordingly, only to get killed, harassed and wrongfully imprisoned. Their actions are a direct result of our government sending mixed signals.

There is another option that we as a country could take. We could keep the references to God and actually apply Biblical principles to our legislation. Unlike the first option, this option would require more than just the stroke of a pen. This option will require action. That's the price for taking a stand. The good news is that America has a long, standing tradition of taking a stand. This should make the implementation of this option easy. All we would have to do is change our view on where we stand to where God stands. This means we no longer take sides with a cultural group or a political party. We now can live up to our name

"United States of America" and unite as one body for the good of all people.

We can begin to implement the second option immediately. It's quite easy: Love and respect God *and* love and respect others by treating them how you want to be treated. It's okay if you don't understand the first half of that premise; simply start applying the second half of it and the first half will become second nature. You don't need to call your State Representative to do that or get 1,000 signatures on a petition. Simply treat the next person you see, whether it's your child, your neighbor or your local cashier at your favorite fast-food restaurant, how you would want that person to act towards you or talk to you. That one act will do more for this country right here right now, than any petition or waiting on Congress to get a vote together.

We get mad at the government without realizing that we *are* the government. The government is made up of people. No people. No government. Armed with that power, change has to start on the individual level. Change your view and you change your destiny and the destiny of this country. We as individuals are this country. As our individual views and actions shift towards the good of all people, the views and courses of actions of our country will seamlessly and naturally shift towards the good of all people as well.

God bless America so that we can truly act as one nation under Him like our founding fathers so eloquently stated and strove for in the words of our Constitution.

I, Larry A. Yff, part of "we the people of the United States", in order to form a more perfect Union, establish Justice, insure domestic tranquility, provide for the common defense, promote the general welfare and secure the Blessings of Liberty to ourselves and our posterity do ordain, establish and approve of this Constitution in its purest, God-respecting form for the benefit of the United States of America.

A TALE OF THREE MEN

There are self-help books, motivational speakers and life coaches whose job is to get you to the point where you can enjoy life. Some make claims that if you apply the teachings of their books you are destined for financial success beyond your wildest dreams; while others say that if you take one of their courses you are guaranteed to live a happier and fuller life. Well, here's *my* claim: If you listen to me or any other "motivational speaker" or buy our books, I can guarantee you will achieve whatever it is that you desire *only* if you take what we give you, *mix* it with a solid knowledge of the Bible and then *apply* it to your everyday life.

Let's compare what two of some industry leaders in this field taught and how applying Bible principles to what they teach gives you the complete package.

Dale Carnegie

1. His book "How to Win Friends and Influence People" has sold more than 15 million copies.
2. His life coaching courses are said to be a "must take" for anyone who wants to succeed in corporate America.
3. It has been said that employers favor a Certificate of Completion from his course over a Bachelor's degree because of its effectiveness in creating top performers.

The core of Dale's work is teaching people how to communicate in such a way that people will give you what you want. Based on the sheer volume of book sales you would have to believe that this is what people crave and strive for in life. Dale's ability to teach people how to communicate effectively has never been questioned. If we take what he did and included Biblical teachings it would look like this:

- ✓ The back of his best seller says if you study this book you will learn how to "make people glad to do what you want." As a Christian I would rather "make people glad doing what *they* want!" His book teaches you how to focus on yourself and on getting what you want. That hints of manipulation and selfishness. As a Christian, if I want someone to *do a desired action for me,* the Bible instructs me to lead by example[1]...not through the mastery of language. To be exact, the Bible says "Treat people how you want to be treated"...not "Convince people to see things your way."
- ✓ The cover of his best seller says "The Only Book You Need to Lead You to Success." Those are powerful words. I agree that it is a book that can lead you to success; but to say "it's the only" book, as a Christian I obviously can't even consider that statement.
- ✓ Wikipedia breaks Dale's coursework and book into about 40 major principles. It reminded me of how in the Bible the religious leaders asked Jesus what the most important law in the Bible was. It was designed to be a trick question because of the huge number of laws and all were considered to be sacred. Jesus said "I can sum up all the laws ever made by God and written by the prophets: the

---

[1] Matthew 7:12

first is to love and respect God and the second is similar and it is that you have to love and respect others because that will show them how to love and respect you. Am I saying Dale's system of listing all the laws and rules for finding success in life was wrong? No. I'm simply saying that he basically took the two laws that were written in the Bible and expanded it for instructional purposes. That in itself is not a bad thing, but if I had the choice of getting success based on a 14 week course or simply applying two laws that the Bible gave us....

Napoleon Hill

1. His book series "Think and Grow Rich" has to date sold over 100 million copies.
2. He spent over 20 years studying the secrets of what makes people successful.
3. He said the secret is "Whatever the mind can conceive and believe it can achieve with positive mental attitude."

Napoleon studied hundreds of successful people to find similarities that he could pinpoint were the keys to their success. His studies were businessmen, presidents, royalty and know actors and athletes. He correctly identified the most visible segment of society that is viewed as being successful...but he left out the not-so-visible, everyday successful people, such as the janitors, nurses, plumbers, valet guy, the warehouse clerk and many others. If we take what he did and included Biblical teachings it would look like this:

✓ The Bible says all men are created equal[2]; making each person's view on success equal. One man views making

$5million a year as success; while another man views surviving past the age of 18 as success. Napoleon had the right concept but failed to view every man as being equal on his quest to determine what success is.

✓ His quote "Whatever the mind can conceive and believe it can achieve with positive mental attitude" is an accurate statement. By his theory, all you have to do is have a vision in life and stay focused and positive and you can achieve it. This gets people excited, but is it possible to stay positive and still fail? For every story of people who had a dream and fought through the chains of addiction and overcame the perils of oppression to find success in a dream fulfilled there are 50 stories where people, by Napoleon's standards, failed. They had the vision and even though the law said "You can't be a lawyer because of the color of your skin…how do you stay positive when on your daily walk to school to get a degree to be a lawyer, you have people looking at you with a deep hatred and spitting on you and hitting you because of your skin color? Once you get a personal understanding of who God is according to the Bible, YOU CANNOT FAIL! Once your very core says "I believe that there is only one God and it's the God in the Bible", you will be able to maintain a positive attitude because your success is now not based on achieving some earthly goal: you have achieved the ultimate goal of being one with the creator of this universe! You have successfully aligned your spiritual and your physical talents and are whole! NOW you set out to be a financial billionaire to show others how to enjoy the

---

[2] Genesis 2:7

Christian life and your attitude is "Let God's will be done." If you don't become that financial billionaire, you understand that that stage in life was simply to make connections for God's calling in your life which is to be behind the scenes as a Christian business advisor. Either way you win because you are doing God's work and that work is more fruitful than any plans you may have had.

In the Bible Jesus says something to the effect of "What good is it to gain the earth and lose your soul?"[3] All humans have a physical side and a spiritual side. How can you really be successful if you only found success in half of who you are? Without success in your spiritual life you have missed the mark. That is where the controversy begins: which spiritual path is the best? That is for you to decide. You have free will. It is my job as a Christian is to show you how to enjoy life and find success in everything you do not only through my books and talks, but by my actions. I agree with Napoleon that you can achieve anything you put your mind to and I understand the rationale behind Dale breaking down the basic human principles. My view and there's differ only because I know I can do all things through Christ who strengthens me…not by having a positive attitude or learning techniques that teach you to be nice to people just to get what you want in life.

---

[3] Luke 9:25

Personal Development Notes

Personal Development Notes

Personal Development Notes

Personal Development Notes

Personal Development Notes

Made in the USA
Columbia, SC
09 May 2022